Building a Healthy Diet with the 5 Food Groups

On My Plate

Building a Healthy Diet with the 5 Food Groups

On My Plate

Building a Healthy Diet with the 5 Food Groups

Kim Etingoff

Mason Crest

Mason Crest
450 Parkway Drive, Suite D
Broomall, PA 19008
www.masoncrest.com

Printed and bound in the United States of America.

First printing
9 8 7 6 5 4 3 2 1

Series ISBN: 978-1-4222-3094-7
ISBN: 978-1-4222-3095-4
ebook ISBN: 978-1-4222-8786-6

Library of Congress Cataloging-in-Publication Data

Etingoff, Kim, author.
  Building a healthy diet with the 5 food groups / Kim Etingoff.
    pages cm. — (On my plate : building a healthy diet with the 5 food groups)
  Audience: Ages 9+.
  Audience: Grades 4 to 6.
  ISBN 978-1-4222-3095-4 (hardback) — ISBN 978-1-4222-3094-7 (series) — ISBN 978-1-4222-8786-6 (ebook) 1. Diet–Juvenile literature. 2. Food habits—Juvenile literature. 3. Health—Juvenile literature. I. Title.
  RA784.E816 2015
  613.2—dc23
                        2014010544

Contents

KEY ICONS TO LOOK FOR:

Text-Dependent Questions: These questions send the reader back to the text for more careful attention to the evidence presented there.

Words to Understand: These words with their easy-to-understand definitions will increase the reader's understanding of the text, while building vocabulary skills.

Series Glossary of Key Terms: This back-of-the book glossary contains terminology used throughout this series. Words found here increase the reader's ability to read and comprehend higher-level books and articles in this field.

Research Projects: Readers are pointed toward areas of further inquiry connected to each chapter. Suggestions are provided for projects that encourage deeper research and analysis.

Sidebars: This boxed material within the main text allows readers to build knowledge, gain insights, explore possibilities, and broaden their perspectives by weaving together additional information to provide realistic and holistic perspectives.

Introduction

Most of us would agree that building healthy bodies and minds is a critical component of future success in school, work, and life. Providing our bodies with adequate and healthy nutrition in childhood sets the stage for both optimal learning and healthy habits in adulthood. Research suggests that the epidemic of overweight and obesity in young children leads to a large medical and financial burden, both for individuals and society. Children who are overweight and obese are more likely to become overweight or obese adults, and they are also at increased risk for a range of diseases.

Developing healthy eating and fitness habits in childhood is one of the most important gifts we can all provide to children in our homes and workplaces—but as any parent can attest, this is not always an easy task! Children are surrounded with both healthy and unhealthy eating options in their homes, schools, and in every restaurant or store they visit. Glossy marketing of food and meals is ubiquitous in media of all types, impacting both children's and adults' eating choices. As a result of the multiple influences on eating choices, from infancy through adulthood, we all benefit from additional support in making healthy choices.

Just as eating and fitness can become habits in adulthood, personal decision-making in childhood is critical to developing healthy habits. Providing healthy options and examples are a starting point, which can support children's healthy habits, but children also benefit from understanding the rationale for eating reasonable portions of healthy foods. Parents, teachers, and others often communicate messages through their words and actions—but books can provide more detailed information and pictures.

Building on this need for developing informed consumers, the ON MY PLATE series provides elementary school children with an informative yet fun introduction to their eating options. Beginning with an introduction to the five food groups, children can learn about what they ideally will have on their own plate and in their mouths. Tips are provided for choosing healthy snacks. And children will understand the importance of eating a range of foods. These books empower our children to make healthy decisions for themselves.

An additional benefit of this series may be the trickle-up effect for parents. Even if we all *know* the importance of making healthy choices for meals and snacks, there's nothing like a child *reminding us* why this is important. When our children start citing the long-term consequences of our dietary choices, we tend to listen!

Here's to developing healthy eating habits today!

Lisa Albers Prock, MD, MPH
Developmental Behavioral Pediatrician, Boston Children's Hospital
Assistant Professor, Harvard Medical School

WORDS TO UNDERSTAND

biology: The structure and makeup of a living thing.

fertilizer: Chemicals and nutrients added to the soil that plants are growing in to help them be healthy.

harvests: Gathers crops after they are done growing.

bacteria: Tiny organisms made up of only a single cell. Some bacteria can make you sick, but others help your body in some way.

Chapter 1

What Are the 5 Food Groups— And Where Do They Come From?

Think of your favorite food. Maybe you love hamburgers. Or watermelon. Or ice cream. You might wish you could eat your favorite food for every meal! You'd never get tired of it. Or at least that's what you think!

Eating the same thing over and over again might be fun for a little while. But eating that way wouldn't do you any good. You'd soon get sick, even if your favorite food were carrots or some other healthy food. If you ate only carrots all the time, you wouldn't be very healthy.

Instead, you need to eat a bunch of different things. The best way to make sure you eat all the different kinds of foods you need is to pay attention to food groups.

We have five food groups. Each food group has different kinds of things your body needs to work right and stay healthy. If you only eat from one or two food groups, your body doesn't get everything it needs to work right.

Fruits and vegetables both come from plants, but they can be different parts of the plant. Both fruits and vegetables are high in vitamins.

MAKE CONNECTIONS

We haven't always grouped food the way we do today. Over time, we've come up with what we think is the best way to help people eat healthy. In the United States, when the government first made up the idea of food groups in 1916, there were five groups, but they were a little different. They were milk and meat, cereals (grains), vegetables and fruits, fats, and sugars. A little later, there were ten food groups. Now there were groups for eggs and water! Plus fruits and vegetables were split up into a few different groups. Then we went back to five again. There's not just one way to look at the foods we need, so we can split them up in different ways. Food groups might even keep changing in the future, as we learn more about nutrition and healthy eating.

The five food groups are fruits, vegetables, grains, dairy, and protein. Each group has foods that come from different places.

FRUITS

Fruits come from plants, and they tend to be sweet. Fruits come in all shapes and sizes. Berries, oranges, bananas, apples, peaches, melons, mangos, and more are all fruits.

There are different kinds of fruit, based on flavor and *biology*. Citrus fruits are sour, like grapefruits, lemons, and oranges. Berries are small and sweet, like raspberries and blueberries.

Fruits come from plants. They hold the plant's seeds. If you ever see seedless fruit, like grapes or oranges, they are probably seedless because scientists and farmers made them that way. They didn't grow that way naturally.

Some fruits grow on trees. Apples, plums, and mangos all grow on trees. Other fruits grow on bushes, like berries. Grapes and melons grow on vines. But they all come from the ground!

Farm crews pick fruit when it's ripe. The farm packages it and sends it to a warehouse. From the warehouse, the fruit travels by truck, train, boat, or plane to the grocery stores where you buy it.

VEGETABLES

Vegetables are also plants, like fruit. They are less sweet, and are often cooked before we eat them.

No two vegetables look alike. There are leafy ones, like lettuce, spinach, and kale. They are actually the leaves of a plant.

Other vegetables are round and fat, like zucchini and tomatoes. Some are seeds, like peas. And broccoli and cauliflower are actually unopened flowers! All of these different things are vegetables.

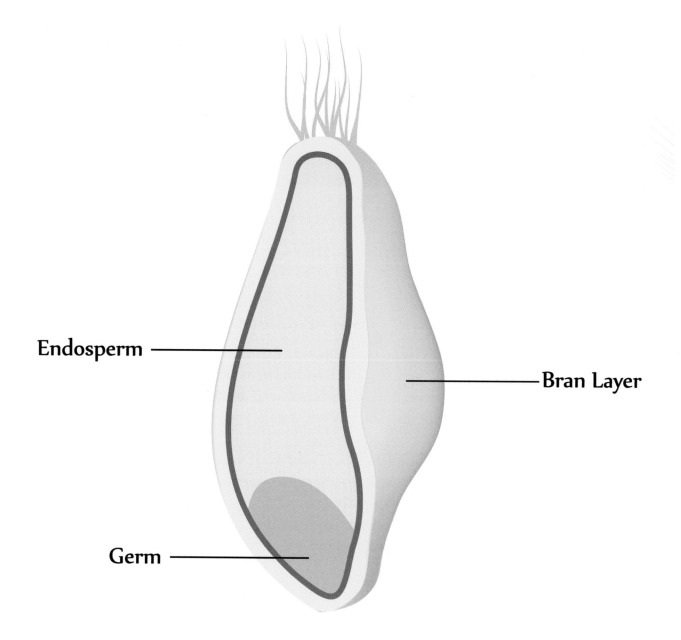

There are three different parts of grains, called the germ, endosperm, and the bran. A food that has all three of these parts in it is called "whole wheat."

MAKE CONNECTIONS

You may have heard that tomatoes are actually fruits. But aren't they vegetables? They're both actually! In terms of biology, anything growing on a plant that has a seed in it is a fruit. Tomatoes are fruits because they have seeds in them. So are eggplants, squash, pumpkins, cucumbers, and peppers. They all have seeds in them. But when you're talking about cooking and eating, tomatoes are vegetables. Vegetables are less sweet than fruits, and they are often cooked before being eaten.

Vegetables, like fruits, are grown on farms. A farmer plants vegetable seeds by hand or with a tractor. Then she takes care of the seedlings when they pop out of the ground. She weeds, gives them food in the form of **fertilizer**, and waters them if the soil gets too dry.

When the vegetables are ready, the farmer **harvests** them. She picks them one by one, or uses a machine to pick lots of them at once.

Then the vegetables are sent to a big warehouse, where they get shipped to grocery stores. All the vegetables (and fruit) you see at the grocery store came from farms around the world.

GRAINS

The third food group is grains. Grains are the seeds of certain kinds of grass plants. They are usually small and hard. They look like seeds!

Oats are a type of grain. So are rice and wheat. Quinoa, spelt, rye, and millet are more types of grains.

You can eat the grains all by themselves. When you make a pot of rice, you're cooking a grain.

But lots of people are more familiar with the foods made out of grains. Wheat is a good example. Not many people eat wheat in its seed form. Most people eat ground-up wheat, which is called flour.

Flour is in a lot of foods. Bread is made out of flour. So are cookies and baked goods. And pasta. And crackers. Wheat is even in things you wouldn't expect, like soy sauce.

Grains fall into two different categories—whole grains and non-whole grains. All grains originally have three different parts, called the germ, the endosperm, and the bran. When grain is harvested on a farm, it is a whole seed. That seed has all three parts in it. If it is sent to stores with all three parts, it is a whole grain.

Often, the farmer will send the grain to a factory. The factory takes out two of the seed's parts. They only leave the endosperm. Grains with only the endosperm are non-whole grains.

Leaving just the endosperm makes the grain last longer. That way, it can be sent to stores around the world. And people can keep the grains for a long time on their shelves.

At a farmers' market, you can buy food directly from the farmers who grow it. This is a great way to help your local community!

Non-whole grain foods are usually lighter in color. White rice and white bread are both made from non-whole grains.

Whole grain foods are darker in color, like brown rice and whole wheat bread. Labels usually say whether a food is a whole grain. Whole grains are healthier for you.

DAIRY

Dairy foods are made from animal milk. Milk itself is a dairy food. Yogurt, cheese, ice cream, and sour cream are also made from milk, so they're dairy too.

Most of the dairy we eat comes from cows. The milk you buy at the store is usually cow's milk. Sometimes people also eat dairy foods made from goats and sheep milk.

Dairy foods come from dairy farms. Farmers have herds of cows (or goats or sheep). They keep them in barns or in fields. They give them food and water. They treat them if they're sick.

They also milk them every day. Cows usually get milked twice a day. In the past, farmers would milk cows by hand. Now, most farmers with more than a cow or two have machines to milk them.

Once the farmers collect the milk, they send it to a factory. Some of the factories put milk in containers and send it to stores. Other factories use the milk to make cheese, yogurt, ice cream, and other dairy foods. To make yogurt, for example, factories mix the milk with special *bacteria* that are safe to eat (and are good for you). The bacteria turn the milk into yogurt. Then the factories send the food on to grocery stores.

You get to choose how much fat you want in a lot of the dairy you eat. Milk comes in different varieties, all with different amounts of fat. Whole milk has the most fat. Two percent milk has a little less, 1 percent even less, and skim has no fat.

You might also see other dairy products that are labeled as reduced-fat, low-fat, or fat-free. All those labels tell you some fat has been taken out of the food.

The USDA recommends that you should get your protein from lots of different foods. Meat, eggs, fish, beans, nuts, and even whole grains all have protein in them!

TEXT-DEPENDENT QUESTIONS

1. What are fruits? What part of the plant do they have inside them?

2. What parts of the plant are are vegetables? How are they different from fruits?

3. How are whole grains different from non-whole-grain foods? What are the benefits of each?

4. Where do dairy products come from? How is milk turned into other dairy products, like yogurt?

5. Lots of people think of meat as the best source of protein. What are three other foods you can get protein from?

PROTEIN

The protein food group has all sorts of foods in it. Eggs count as protein. Meat from any animal, including fish, is a protein. Beans and nuts are also protein.

All of those foods have one thing in common—protein. Protein is a substance in food that keeps us healthy, especially our muscles. Eggs, meat, beans, and nuts all have protein in them.

Protein foods all have something in common, though—they all come from farms, just like every other food.

Meat comes from animal flesh. Beef is cow, pork is pig, and of course, chicken is chicken! Those animals are raised on farms. Farmers raise animals for meat on fields or in pens. Often there are hundreds, thousands, or even millions of animals in one herd or farm!

Most meat animals are sent to feedlots before they become meat. They are fed grain to fatten them up in the feedlots. From the feedlots, the animals go to slaughterhouses. They are killed for meat, and the meat is put into packages. Then the packages are sent to the store.

The eggs we eat almost always come from chickens. Farmers keep lots and lots of chickens in pens in factories. The eggs are usually collected by machines and packaged up into cartons. Like all the rest of the food, eggs are sent to you through the grocery store.

So there you have it: fruits, vegetables, grains, dairy, and protein. Those five food groups add up to a healthy diet. If you eat them all, you'll be well on your way to a healthy and delicious life!

WORDS TO UNDERSTAND

nutrients: A substance in food that you need to grow and live.
digestive system: The parts of your body that work together to break down
food and get the nutrients you need from it.
absorb: Take in.

Chapter 2

Why Do I Need to Eat a Variety of Foods?

Humans, like every other living thing, need certain things to survive and grow. We need food and water to stay alive. If you don't eat, you don't live!

We can't just eat anything, though, and expect to live our best. People need the right foods to stay healthy. The five food groups contain all the things we need to live and be healthy.

NUTRIENTS FOR LIFE

Food has substances called **nutrients** in them. You can probably already name some nutrients, like calcium and vitamin C.

You can't see the nutrients in food. Nutrients are really, really small. But just because they're small, doesn't mean they're not important. They are the reason we eat food in the first place!

Limit these nutrients →

Get enough of these nutrients →

Nutrition facts

Serving size 1 cup (9 oz - 255g)
Servings per container 2

Amount per serving
Calories 485   Calories from fat 220

	% Daily Value*
Total fat 1 oz - 28 g	**32%**
Satured fat 0.5 oz - 14g	38%
Trans fat 0.2 oz - 6g	
Sodium 0.03 oz - 0.9g	**13%**
Total carbohydrate 1.5 oz - 42g	**11%**
Dietary fiber 0 oz - 0g	0%
Sugars 0.2 oz - 6g	
Protein 0.2 oz - 6g	

Vitamin A	**5%**	**Calcium**	**18%**
Vitamin C	**3%**	**Iron**	**6%**

* Percent Daily Value are based on a 2500 calorie diet. Your Daily Value may be higher or lower depending on your calorie need.

Quick Guide to % Daily Value:

5% or less is low

20% or more is high

Most foods in the United States have a "Nutrition Facts" label. This label says how much of each important vitamin or mineral they have.

MAKE CONNECTIONS

Some people take vitamins every day. Vitamins pack in lots of nutrients into a pill. They are fast and easy ways to get many of the nutrients you need in a day. However, vitamins aren't the best way to get the nutrients. You're always better off actually getting your nutrients through food and a healthy diet. But there's no harm in taking a vitamin, especially if you just can't seem to eat enough healthy foods.

Every nutrient helps your body in a different way. Some of them keep your bones strong, while others help you see or think straight. When you eat all the nutrients together, they keep your whole body working the way it should.

Not every food group has a lot of every nutrient. Fruit has a lot of vitamins like vitamins A and C. Fruits don't have much protein or iron though. You need protein and iron as much as you need those vitamins.

You'll have to eat more than just fruit to get all the nutrients you need. Eating meat or beans from the protein group will give you the protein and iron you aren't getting from fruit.

When you eat from all five food groups, you have a balanced diet. (Your diet is made up of the foods you choose to eat.) You eat just enough foods from each group to be healthy.

You have an unbalanced diet when you only eat from a couple food groups. If you only ate dairy all the time, you would have an unbalanced diet. If you only ate fruits and vegetables all the time, without any proteins, dairy, or grains, you would have an unbalanced diet.

Balanced diets keep you healthy and feeling good. You have a lot of energy, and you don't get sick very much. You're strong, and you feel happier.

When you have an unbalanced diet, the opposite happens. You might feel tired all the time, or get sick a lot. You don't look very good and you don't feel very good.

Luckily, all you have to do is start eating better! When you start paying attention to nutrients and food groups, you'll start eating healthier. And then you'll be healthier!

VITAMINS

Vitamins are substances our body doesn't make, although our bodies need them to work right. Other living things make vitamins. We have to eat those living things to get the vitamins.

People have named vitamins with letters—vitamins A, B, C, D, E, and K. Plus, there are eight different kinds of vitamin B.

To be really healthy, you need all of those vitamins on a regular basis. Different food groups are high in different vitamins. You should eat all the food groups to get enough of all the vitamins.

Plants absorb minerals from the ground. When you eat the plants, in the form of fruits, grains, and vegetables, your body can use those minerals.

MAKE CONNECTIONS

Allergies can get in the way of eating all five food groups. Mostly, people are allergic to one or two foods, like peanuts or shellfish. In more extreme cases, someone is allergic to a whole category of foods, like dairy. Food intolerances can also get in the way of eating from the five food groups. Someone has a food intolerance if her body can't digest that food properly. A lot of people have intolerances to dairy and gluten, a substance found in some grains like wheat and barley.

If you have an allergy or food intolerance, don't worry! You can still eat a balanced diet; you just have to be a little more careful. If you can't eat dairy, you're missing out on fat, protein, and some vitamins. You can make them up, though, by making sure you eat other foods that are high in the nutrients you're missing. Eat more beans or meat, and fruits and veggies!

Fruits and vegetables tend to have a lot of most of the vitamins. Eggs have vitamin B, D, and K. Meat has some of the kinds of vitamin B. Most foods have at least a few vitamins in them.

Some of the foods you find in the store have vitamins added to them. Breakfast cereal boxes often say they are "fortified" with iron or vitamin D. Fortified means the food has had vitamins or minerals added to it. Orange juice often has added calcium. Buying foods that have extra vitamins in them helps make sure you're getting all the vitamins you need.

MINERALS

People also need tiny amounts of nutrients called minerals. Unlike vitamins, minerals come from non-living things. Plants suck them up through the soil, and other animals eat those plants. But like vitamins, our bodies can't make minerals, so we have to get them through food.

Different minerals do different things in your body. Calcium, found in dairy foods and dark green vegetables, keeps bones strong. Iron keeps our blood healthy, and helps our bodies have the energy they need to work and play, think and learn. Beans, dark leafy greens, and soybeans have a lot of iron in them. Sodium keeps the water in your body balanced, so we don't have too much or too little. Sodium is another word for salt. If you eat *too much* salt, though, that's not healthy either.

Food has lots of other minerals we need too. Some of the other minerals we need are potassium, phosphorous, magnesium, zinc, copper, and iodine. Each of these minerals does different things to keep our bodies healthy. We only need really tiny amounts of all those minerals. However, without them, people get sick.

CARBOHYDRATES

People only need to eat very small amounts of vitamins and minerals. We need to eat more

Starches and fiber are made of long chains of sugars. For this reason, they are sometimes called "complex sugars." They can be found in lots of different foods, like pasta.

of three other nutrients. We call them macronutrients. Macro means big. We need bigger amounts of macronutrients to be healthy.

Macronutrients give us energy. Think of a car. You have to put gasoline in the car or it won't go anywhere. Macronutrients are like gasoline, but for people. They provide the fuel that keeps us going, so we can walk, work, play, and even breathe and pump blood!

One buil the macronutrients we need is carbohydrates (or carbs). There are three different kinds of carbohydrates: sugar, starch, and dietary fiber.

MAKE CONNECTIONS

When you think of the protein food group, you might first think of meat. You'd be right that meat has a lot of protein. But other foods have plenty of protein too, like beans, tofu, eggs, and also whole grains. Many people these days are vegetarians and don't eat meat. If you're a vegetarian, you don't have to worry about not getting enough protein, as long as you make sure to eat a variety of other foods with protein in them.

Sugar gives us quick energy. It's an easy form of energy for your body to use. Lots of foods have sugar in them naturally. Fruits are the main food group that has natural sugar in it. Health problems happen when we eat too much added sugar, though. Cereals have tons of added sugar. So do juice drinks, cakes, cookies, and ice cream. Too much sugar is bad for the body, but we do need some.

Starches are a little harder for our body to use than sugar is. They have to be broken down by the *digestive system* first. Then they can be used for energy over a longer period of time than sugar. Grains have lots of starch in them. So do vegetables.

Fiber is the third kind of carbohydrate. The body can't digest fiber. Instead, fiber is important because it keeps the digestive system healthy. Fiber keeps your food moving through your intestines. That's a good thing. If your food just sat there inside you, without moving through the parts of your digestive system, you would feel sick. Your stomach would hurt. Your body wouldn't be able to absorb nutrients from your food the way it's supposed to.

Whole grains have the most fiber. Fruits and vegetables also have some fiber too. You need to eat some of these foods every day.

FATS

The second macronutrient we need is fat. Fat is really important. It helps young people

RESEARCH PROJECT

These days, you hear a lot about how unhealthy fat is and how people are eating too much of it. But not all fat is bad! You learned that the best fats for you to eat are unsaturated fats. Use the Internet to look up some foods that are good sources of unsaturated fats. Do you already eat some of these foods? Now look up what foods might be high in saturated fats and trans fats. Do you eat many of these foods? How can you cut down the amount of saturated and trans fats you're eating?

Eating a healthy, balanced diet means eating food from many different food groups. Some foods might not have vitamins or nutrients that another food has, so you should eat a little of each.

grow. It gives the body a lot of energy. It also helps the body take in vitamins. Without fat, the body wouldn't be able to **absorb** some vitamins, even if we ate a lot of them.

Meat, nuts, and dairy have the most fat. Butter, for example, has a lot of fat. Whole milk has more fat than skim milk.

Like carbohydrates, fat comes in different kinds. Unsaturated fat is the healthiest kind of fat. Unsaturated fat is in foods like avocados, oil, and nuts. This kind of fat keeps your body healthy, especially your heart. Saturated fat and trans fats are less healthy. They can make your heart sick if you eat too much of them. Saturated fats are found in meat and dairy. Trans fats are the fats in baked goods and snack foods.

TEXT-DEPENDENT QUESTIONS

1. Why is it important to eat lots of different kinds of food? For example, why shouldn't you eat all fruit, even though fruit is healthy?

2. What are vitamins? What are some foods where you can find lots of vitamins?

3. What are minerals? How are they different from vitamins?

4. What's the difference between a macronutrient and a micronutrient? What are the three macronutrients?

5. What macronutrient do you get most of your energy from?

PROTEIN

Finally, the third macronutrient is protein. For young people who are still growing, protein is really important. Protein helps young people grow and develop. Without protein, you wouldn't become a healthy adult. Protein also makes muscles strong and healthy. People trying to build up muscles eat a lot of protein.

This macronutrient is also a backup source of energy. When your body uses up the energy it has from carbohydrates and fats, it turns to protein.

You can probably guess which food group has the most protein—the protein group! Meat, beans, eggs, and nuts have a lot of protein in them.

PUTTING IT ALL TOGETHER

As you can see, we need a lot of nutrients from food! Each food group has different nutrients in them.

Now you can see why just eating carrots every day wouldn't be very good for you. Carrots have a lot of vitamins A, C, and K. They have some potassium and fiber. They're pretty healthy because they have so many nutrients.

But carrots don't have all the nutrients you need. They're missing lots of other nutrients. You wouldn't get much vitamin B or D if you only ate carrots. You wouldn't get protein, fat, calcium, or iron. You wouldn't feel very well missing out on all those nutrients.

In general, fruits and vegetables have lots of vitamins and minerals. If you only ate fruits and vegetables, though, you would be missing out, especially on nutrients like protein and fat.

So, you have to eat other food groups too. Dairy, meat, or beans will give you protein and fat. Grains will give you carbohydrates, protein, and some more vitamins and minerals. Put them all together, and you have a healthy, balanced diet!

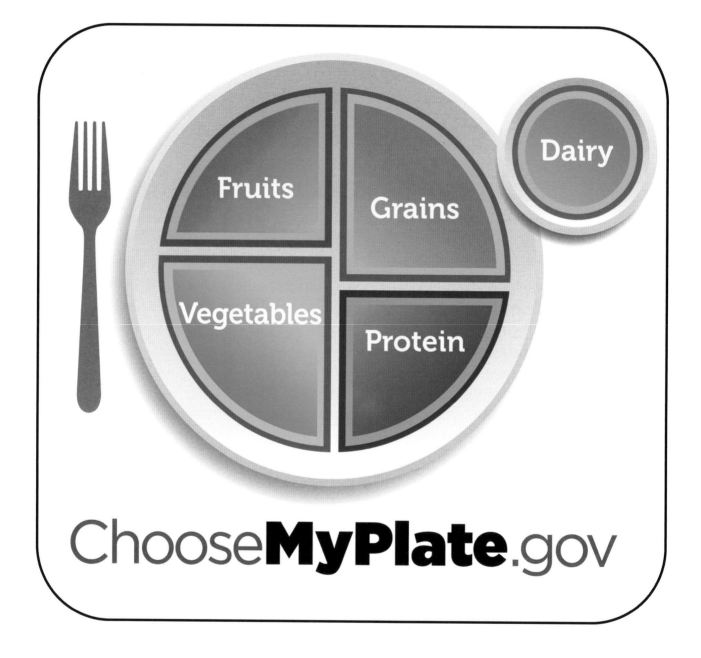

ChooseMyPlate.gov

Chapter

3

Putting the 5 Food Groups on My Plate

So now you know you need to eat food from all five food groups. But how much from each food group should you eat? Figuring out what to eat to get enough of each nutrient can get tricky. Luckily, there's a tool to help you out when you get confused. The tool is called MyPlate. The United States government created MyPlate to help people eat healthier. Knowing how to use MyPlate will help you make the right food decisions.

UNDERSTANDING MYPLATE

MyPlate is basically a picture. It's a picture of a plate with a meal on it. The plate shows you how much of each food group you should eat every day.

The plate is divided into four sections, plus a cup in the corner. Each section is labeled

You should eat a little more vegetables than fruit each day, but it's still important that you eat some of each.

with a food group. The size of the sections shows you how much of each food group you should eat.

On the left half of the plate are fruits and vegetables. If you divided your plate into four sections, each section would be about one quarter of your plate. A little bit more than one-quarter should be vegetables. A little bit less than one-quarter should be fruits. Fruits are red and vegetables are green. The vegetable section is a little bit bigger than the fruit section. That tells you that you should eat slightly more vegetables than fruits.

On the other half of the plate are grains and protein. Grains are orange, and protein is purple. One-quarter of your plate should be grains, and the last quarter of your plate should be protein.

Up in the corner is a blue circle section labeled dairy. It shows you a glass of milk. The plate and the glass together show all five food groups.

USING MYPLATE

Imagine a meal you're eating. Maybe it's a big dinner with your family. Your family is serving brown rice, chicken, broccoli, and fruit salad.

With MyPlate, you can figure how much of each food to eat. The easiest thing to do is to divide your plate into four equal sections in your head. Then add food to each section. MyPlate tells you one section should be grain. The brown rice goes in one section. One section should be protein, so you add the chicken to that one. You also know from MyPlate that the other half of your plate should be fruits and vegetables. Add vegetables to slightly more than half of the rest of your plate. The section that remains is for fruit. Don't forget to pour yourself a glass of milk for dairy!

This is the easiest way to understand MyPlate. But you probably don't always eat this way. You might not eat all five food groups at every meal. Or you might not separate out each food group on your plate in one meal.

You can also think about MyPlate in terms of how you eat in a whole day. Let's say you eat oatmeal for breakfast. You add some fresh strawberries on top. You drink a glass of orange juice too.

You just ate some grains (the oatmeal). You also ate a lot of fruit. The strawberries and the orange juice both count as fruits, as long as the juice was 100 percent juice.

You didn't eat any vegetables, dairy, or protein. Does that mean you're eating unhealthy? Not at all! You can't always eat every food group at every meal. But you do need to eat vegetables, dairy, and protein sometime during your day. If you don't, then your diet won't be balanced for the day.

So for lunch you could choose to eat some vegetable soup. You might also have a piece

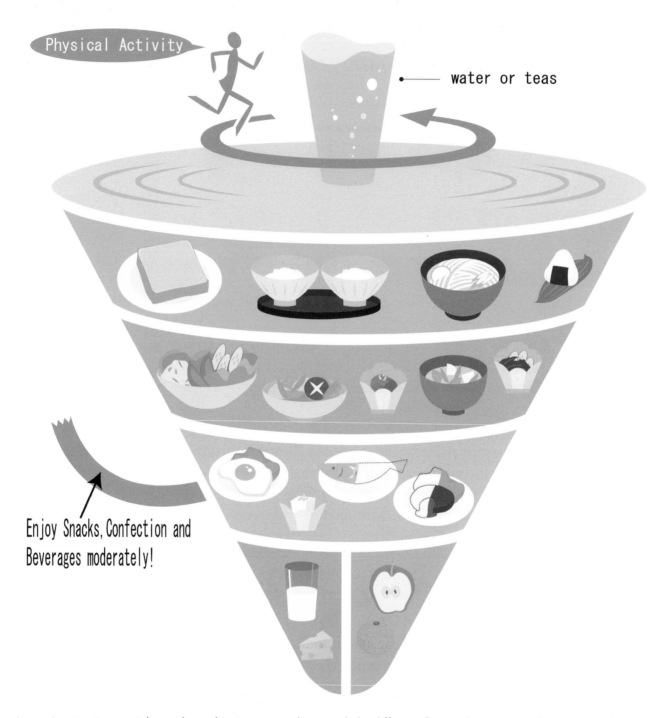

Physical Activity

water or teas

Enjoy Snacks, Confection and Beverages moderately!

Japan's spinning top shows how the Japanese diet is a little different from what you might see in a Western country like the United States, but both countries recommend physical activity and a balanced diet.

of whole-wheat toast with peanut butter and a glass of milk. You just added vegetables to your day. Plus, you got more grains (toast), protein (peanut butter), and dairy (milk).

For dinner your family makes a stir-fry. The stir-fry has chicken, broccoli, and brown rice. This time, all the ingredients are mixed up together. You can still use MyPlate to imagine what would happen if you divided up that stir-fry into different sections on your plate. Imagining the sections helps you figure out how much of each ingredient you should eat. You shouldn't just eat brown rice and chicken without the broccoli, for example. Then you aren't eating any vegetables.

HOW MUCH DO I EAT?

You're still missing one more important piece of information—how much of each food to eat!

Lots of people tend to overeat. They eat more food than they need. When you eat too much all the time, you don't feel very well. You also start to gain weight, which is dangerous for your health.

The U.S. government also has guides about how much food to eat. How much you need depends on who you are. Men tend to need to eat more than women. Teens and adults need to eat more than young kids. People who are more active need to eat more.

The key to understanding how much you need to eat is calories. Calories are a measure of how much energy a food has.

One serving of meat is only about the size of a computer mouse, and a serving of carbohydrates is half a bagel or two slices of white bread. Most Americans eat a lot more than one serving at meals, though!

A food that has 10 calories doesn't give you a lot of energy. Ten calories won't keep you going for very long. A food that has 250 calories has a lot more energy. That food will keep you going longer.

You don't want to eat too many calories. Then you'll start to gain weight. You also don't want to eat too few calories, unless you need to lose weight for health reasons. Without enough calories, you won't have enough energy for your day.

The MyPlate website has a Daily Food Plan page. You can look up how much of each food group you need, based on how many calories you should be eating every day.

RESEARCH PROJECT

Compare MyPlate to the other diet recommendations charts in this chapter. Now, go online and see if you can find food pyramids or charts from any other countries. How are these charts similar to the United States' MyPlate? How are they different? Why do you think other countries have different foods that they recommend? Why do you think some countries include physical activity on their food diagrams, but others don't?

TEXT-DEPENDENT QUESTIONS

1. What do the five sections of the MyPlate diagram represent?

2. Do you need to match the foods you eat at every meal to the MyPlate diagram to be healthy?

3. Why is the amount of food that you eat important? What are two factors that affect how much you need to eat?

4. What happens if you eat more calories than you use in a day?

5. What's one example of a serving of carbohydrates? How about a serving of dairy?

If you're ten years old and very active, you might need 2,200 calories a day. The MyPlate website will tell you just how much of each food group you need to eat. You'll need 7 ounces of grain, 3 cups of vegetables, 2 cups of fruit, 3 cups of dairy, and 6 ounces of protein foods.

Now you need to figure out how much an ounce of grain is and a cup of dairy! Luckily, the website also helps you find that information too. Here's some help:

- 1 ounce of grain equals a one-half cup brown rice, 3 cups of popcorn, or 1 slice of bread.
- 1 cup of vegetables equals a big pile of raw spinach, one medium baked potato, or about 15 baby carrots.
- 1 cup of fruit equals a banana, a half cup of orange juice, or a quarter cup of raisins.
- 1 cup of dairy equals 8 ounces of milk, one 8-ounce container of yogurt, or one-third cup shredded cheddar cheese.
- 1 ounce of protein equals 3 slices of deli ham, about 12 almonds, or a quarter cup of cooked black beans.

Drive-Thru
Clearance 9 Feet

BOTH
LANES
OPEN
ANY SIZE
soft drink or sweet tea
$1

WORDS TO UNDERSTAND

obesity: A health condition in which you are very overweight—your body has so much extra fat that it can hurt your quality of life.

processed: Food that has had parts added or removed.

Chapter 4

Fast Foods, Snacks, and the 5 Food Groups

It's hard enough to eat all five food groups and have a balanced diet during meals at home. Eating out, especially when you're eating fast food, and eating snacks is even harder!

Luckily, there are lots of ways to get your five food groups in even when you're eating less-than-healthy fast food and snacks.

FAST-FOOD UPGRADES

Fast food is a big part of many people's lives. At least one out of four young people eat fast food every single day.

Yet fast food is some of the least healthy food out there. Fast food has tons of calories—

Many fast-food restaurants have some healthy options available. If you're eating fast food, choose your meal carefully!

but it doesn't have many nutrients. Calories without any nutrients with them are called empty calories.

Fast food has lots and lots of unhealthy fat, salt, and sugar. All three of those things cause health problems like heart disease and **obesity**.

Fast food also doesn't include all five food groups. Fast food has a lot of protein, especially meat. It also has a lot of grains, like hamburger buns and the coating on chicken nuggets. However, there aren't many whole grains on fast food menus, which are a lot healthier for you than **processed** grains. And there aren't many fruits, vegetables, or dairy.

Some fast food restaurants are realizing that people want to eat healthier. These restaurants offer some choices that are a little healthier. Some of them even have vegetables in them!

You may have to be a little creative if you want to eat as many food groups as possible at fast food restaurants. Always choose more vegetables, if that's a choice. You should also choose whole-grain foods, like whole-wheat bread. Choose milk or water, not soda. And try and pick healthy side dishes, like apple slices or fruit salad.

What would a healthier fast food meal look like? You could order a sub on a whole-wheat roll with lots of veggies along with meat and cheese. And drink water. Or you could get a small hamburger with apple slices on the side and milk.

Some fast food restaurants offer salads. To get lots of veggies, you could order a salad with grilled chicken or beans for some protein. Oil-based salad dressings like Italian or vinaigrette are better for you than creamy dressings.

It's okay to snack throughout the day. It might even help to keep you from eating meals that are too big! But make sure you're snacking on healthy foods instead of junk foods.

If you choose to eat fast food with more food groups, you're taking a step in the right direction with your health. You'll start to feel better and have more energy. You'll also thank yourself later in life, when you're still fit and healthy from that balanced diet!

SNACKING BETTER

Snacks are a great way to eat some of the food groups you're missing from the rest of your meals during the day. You may not eat much fruit for breakfast, lunch, or dinner. But you can always add in some fruit for a snack between meals.

Snacks also keep your energy up during the day. As long as you don't eat too much for a snack, they're great ways to get you from meal to meal.

Not all snacks are equal, though. Many snacks are unhealthy and aren't worth eating. They just add empty calories to your day, along with lots of fat, sugar, and salt. Cookies, chips, and candy are not good choices for snacks. None of those snacks really belong to any food group—they're just junk.

Snacks don't have to be just about chips and cookies, though. You can make and eat tasty, healthy snacks too! You'll find you don't even miss those junk snacks.

Try to eat snacks that have more than one food group. Be creative and add two or more food groups together.

Make a smoothie with fruit and milk or 100 percent juice. Add any kind of fruit you like, such as bananas, strawberries, blueberries, and mango. Add in some yogurt for extra dairy, or peanut butter for some protein.

When you make popcorn yourself with an air popper or on the stove, it can be a very healthy snack, but microwave popcorn and movie theater popcorn are usually high in fat and salt.

Apples and cheese slices also make a great snack. Apples and peanut butter are another good choice.

Get some extra veggies into your day with snacks. Cut up carrots, peppers, cucumbers, celery, and more into sticks. Then dip them into a yogurt dip or hummus, which is made out of chickpeas and counts as protein.

Popcorn is a healthy grain snack. As long as you don't load it up with butter and salt, popcorn is great. You can pop loose kernels on the stove or in a brown paper bag in the microwave.

In general, the more fruits, vegetables, and whole grains, the better. Those are the things we tend not to eat enough of during the rest of the day. Healthy snacks can help you fill in the gaps.

HEALTHY EATING TIPS

Getting enough healthy foods is hard for a lot of people. Eating enough fruits, vegetables, and whole grains is especially hard. We're used to eating lots of junk food. You'll be much happier and healthier if you eat a balanced diet, though.

The United States Department of Agriculture (USDA), the organization that made MyPlate, has lots of tips for eating each food group. Here are some of them, from the MyPlate website.

Fruits

- Keep a bowl of whole fruit on the table, counter, or in the refrigerator.
- Buy fruits that are dried, frozen, and canned (in water or 100% juice) as well as fresh, so that you always have a supply on hand.
- When choosing canned fruits, select fruit canned in 100% fruit juice or water rather than syrup.
- At breakfast, top your cereal with bananas or peaches; add blueberries to pancakes; drink 100% orange or grapefruit juice. Or mix fresh fruit with plain fat-free or low-fat yogurt.
- At lunch, pack a tangerine, banana, or grapes to eat, or choose fruits from a salad bar. Individual containers of fruits like peaches or applesauce are easy and convenient.
- For dessert, have baked apples, pears, or a fruit salad.

MAKE CONNECTIONS

Diabetes is a disease that means there is something wrong with a chemical called insulin that your body normally produces. Insulin helps handle the amount of sugar in your blood. Without insulin working right, you end up with too much or too little sugar in your blood.

There are two kinds of diabetes. Type I diabetes isn't caused by diet. People with Type I diabetes get it when they are young, and they have to give themselves insulin shots. Their bodies can't produce any insulin. Type II diabetes often happens to people who are overweight and who have unbalanced diets. People with both kinds of diabetes have to take care of themselves more carefully and take medications so the disease doesn't lead to other problems. They have to watch their diets carefully.

Whole-grain cereals are an easy way to get more whole grains in your diet. They're also usually high in many different vitamins and minerals.

Vegetables

- Stock up on frozen vegetables for quick and easy cooking in the microwave.
- Buy vegetables that are easy to prepare.
- Use a microwave to quickly "zap" vegetables.
- Vary your veggie choices to keep meals interesting.
- Try crunchy vegetables, raw or lightly steamed.
- Buy canned vegetables labeled "reduced sodium," "low sodium," or "no salt added."
- Plan some meals around a vegetable main dish, such as a vegetable stir-fry or soup.
- Include a green salad with your dinner every night.
- Include chopped vegetables in pasta sauce or lasagna.
- Order a veggie pizza with toppings like mushrooms, green peppers, and onions, and ask for extra veggies.

- Many vegetables taste great with a dip or dressing. Try a low-fat salad dressing with raw broccoli, red and green peppers, celery sticks, or cauliflower.
- Use chopped vegetables as afternoon snacks.

Whole Grains

- For a change, try brown rice or whole-wheat pasta.
- Snack on ready-to-eat, whole-grain cereals, such as toasted oat cereal, instead of eating chips.
- Add whole-grain flour or oatmeal when making cookies or other baked treats.
- Try 100% whole-grain snack crackers.
- Popcorn, a whole grain, can be a healthy snack if made with little or no added salt and butter.
- Read the ingredient list on cereals or snack food packages and choose those with whole grains at the top of the list.

IT'S YOUR CHOICE

Healthy eating might seem like it has a lot of rules. One way to make it simpler is to just focus on food groups. The more variety of foods you get, from all five food groups, the better! Keep the MyPlate picture in your head. It will help you know that you're getting the right amounts of each food group. If you do, you'll get more nutrients you need, like vitamins and minerals. You'll have a balanced diet, and a healthy life.

Healthy eating isn't just something adults tell you to do. Healthy eating really makes a difference! You feel better when you make healthy food choices. You have more energy and can do more of the things you love.

You'll also stay healthy. You won't get all those illnesses that come from a bad diet, like type II diabetes, heart disease, and stroke. You'll stay a healthy weight, and you may even catch fewer colds and other "bugs" that go around your school.

Get in the habit of making healthy choices. Eat a lot of different foods instead of always eating one thing all the time. Taking care of your body is one of the best things you can do for yourself!

Getting older means you'll be making more and more decisions for yourself. You'll be choosing how you want to live the rest of your life. How you eat is an important decision to make.

The decision is yours! Start making some small choices and build up from there. Eat one more fruit or vegetable every day. Try new things. Then add more fruits and veggies, and some whole grains. Pretty soon, you'll be eating healthy and feeling great.

RESEARCH PROJECT

Go online and look up some ideas or recipes for healthy snacks, and pick one that you think you'd like. The next time you get food, buy the ingredients to make it! Do you like the snack you picked? Could you get into the habit of eating it more? What makes the snack you picked more healthy than junk food snacks like chips or cookies?

Find Out More

ONLINE

KidsHealth: Food Guide Pyramid Becomes a Plate
kidshealth.org/kid/stay_healthy/food/pyramid.html#cat117

KidsHealth: Recipes and Cooking
kidshealth.org/kid/recipes/#cat117

Kids Eat Right
www.eatright.org/kids

MyPlate.gov
www.choosemyplate.gov

Nourish Interactive
www.nourishinteractive.com

IN BOOKS

Borget-Spaniol, Megan. *Eating Right with MyPlate: Healthy Eating.* Minneapolis, Minn.: Bellweather Media, 2012.

Claybourne, Anna. *Healthy Eating; Diet and Nutrition.* Portsmouth, N.H.: Heinemann, 2008.

Graimes, Nicola. *Kids' Fun and Healthy Cookbook.* New York: DK Publishing, 2007.

Paris, Stephanie. *Straight Talk: The Truth About Food.* Huntington Beach, Calif.: Teacher Created Materials, 2013.

Wilson, Charles and Eric Schlosser. *Chew On This: Everything You Don't Want to Know About Fast Food.* New York: Houghton Mifflin, 2006.

Series Glossary of Key Terms

Carbohydrates: The types of molecules in food that we get most of our energy from. Foods like sugars and grains are especially high in carbohydrates.

Dairy: Milk or foods that are made from milk.

Diabetes: A disease where the body can't use sugar to produce energy correctly.

Diet: All the foods and nutrients that you normally eat.

Energy: The power stored in food that lets your body move around and carry out other body functions.

Farm: A place where plants and animals are grown and raised to produce food.

Fast food: Food designed to be ready for the customer as fast as possible. Usually it's more expensive and less healthy than fresh food, but it is very convenient.

Fiber: Tough parts of plant foods that your body can't digest. Fiber helps your digestive system function normally.

Fruits: A food group that includes the edible parts of plants that contain the seeds. They are often colorful and have a sweet flavor.

Grains: The seeds of various kinds of grass plant. Grains include rice, wheat, corn, and many others. They are high in carbohydrates and fiber, and can be stored for a long time.

Harvest: The process of or time when crops are gathered.

Local foods: Foods that are grown close to where they are eaten, so they don't have to be transported very far.

Minerals: Materials found naturally in metals or rocks. Our bodies need certain minerals in very small quantities.

Nutrients: Any part of food that our body uses in some way to survive and stay healthy.

Obesity: A state of being so overweight that it's bad for your health.

Organic: A way of producing food in which no genetic modifications, harmful pesticides, or hormones can be used.

Protein: The chemical parts of food that your body uses to build muscles and perform certain body processes. If your body runs out of carbohydrates and fat, it will start using protein for energy.

Vegetables: Plant foods that are usually made of the flower, stem, leaf, or root of a plant. They are usually high in fiber and certain nutrients.

Vitamins: Certain kinds of molecules that your body cannot produce. Instead, you need to get them in your diet to stay healthy.

Index

About the Author & Consultant

Kim Etingoff lives in Boston, Massachusetts. She spends part of her time working on farms, and enjoys writing on topics related to health and nutrition.

Dr. Lisa Prock is a developmental behavioral pediatrician at Children's Hospital (Boston) and Harvard Medical School. She attended college at the University of Chicago, medical school at Columbia University, and received a master's degree in public health from the Harvard School of Public Health. Board-certified in general pediatrics and developmental behavioral pediatrics, she currently is Clinical Director of Developmental and Behavioral Pediatrics and Consultant to the Walker School, a residential school serving children in foster care. Dr. Prock has combined her clinical interests in child development and international health with advocacy for children in medical, residential, and educational settings since 1991. She has worked in Cambodia teaching pediatrics and studying tuberculosis epidemiology; and in Eastern Europe visiting children with severe neurodevelopmental challenges in orphanages. She has co-authored numerous original publications and articles for families. She is a also nonprofit board member for organizations and has received numerous local and national awards for her work with children and families.

Picture Credits